The 1930s family car. The Ford Eight (horsepower) model Y saloon was the first truly Dagenham-designed model. First introduced in 1932, it was priced at £100 in 1935 and over 220,000 8 horsepower cars were sold up to 1939. The engine was a 939 cc side-valve unit with three-speed synchromesh gearbox and rod-operated brakes.

MOTOR CARS OF THE 1930s

Ian Dussek

Shire Publications Ltd

CONTENTS

Motoring in the 1930s 3

The British popular car 10

American and European cars 16

Sports cars 21

Cars for the nobility and gentry 29

Further reading 32

Places to visit 32

Copyright © 1989 by Ian Dussek. First published 1989. Shire Album 237. ISBN 0 85263 981 3.

Printed in Great Britain by C. I. Thomas & Sons (Haverfordwest) Ltd, Press Buildings, Merlins Bridge, Haverfordwest, Dyfed SA61 1XF.

British Library Cataloguing in Publication Data: Dussek, Ian. Motor Cars of the 1930s. 1. Cars, history. I. Title. 629. 2'2̈22'09. ISBN 0-85263-981-3

Editorial Consultant: Michael E. Ware, Curator of the National Motor Museum, Beaulieu.

ACKNOWLEDGEMENTS
The photographs, including the cover, and much assistance in the production of this album were kindly provided by the National Motor Museum, Beaulieu, Hampshire.

Cover: *The Rolls Bentley 3½ litre sports saloon is typical of many of the luxury motor cars built in Britain during the 1930s. Very different from their great racing predecessors of the 1920s, the Bentley 3½ and 4¼ litre models were basically Rolls-Royces with raised performance, extolled in their publicity as 'silent sports cars'.*

Below: *1930s dream car. The D8-120 Delage, as envisaged by the body stylist, was better in fantasy than in fact. It weighed some 2 tonnes and, despite its magnificent exhaust system, could barely achieve 90 mph (140 km/h) from its eight-cylinder engine.*

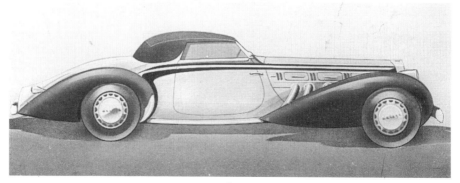

Riley produced a range of successful and very rapid two-seaters, supplemented by a range of unusual four-seater sports saloons, such as this 1934 9 horsepower Kestrel. The flowing tail treatment was subsequently copied by several manufacturers.

MOTORING IN THE 1930s

The motor car grew up in the 1930s. It broke away from its horse-drawn antecedents and developed its own identity. The development was not only technical, but commercial, legal and social. The car was no longer a plaything for the wealthy, but an economic fact of life.

In 1930 cars were constructed round a chassis, predominantly by hand. Bodies were separate, with rudimentary all-weather protection. Braking systems were mechanical, gearboxes non-synchromesh, suspension systems were basic and some wheels were still fabricated from wood. In Britain they travelled on roads only slightly improved from horse-drawn times, at a maximum legal speed of 20 mph (32 km/h). Although Ford and Austin pioneered cheap motoring, cars were by no means common and few suburban British houses incorporated a garage.

By 1940 a revolution had taken place. Unitary construction, that is the com-bination of steel body and chassis, was established, as were mass-produced saloon bodies, hydraulic braking, synchromesh gearboxes, independent suspension and full electric systems including semaphore indicators and sometimes even heaters and radios. The cars of the late 1930s can be recognised as basically similar to the cars of the present day. They travelled on better roads (and even on a few bypasses constructed to relieve traffic jams in the old market towns) at unlimited speeds, except in built-up areas where a 30 mph (48 km/h) limit was enforced by a zealous constabulary. Traffic lights and pedestrian crossings marked by Belisha beacons proliferated. The local mechanics, blacksmiths and chemists who had sold petrol were replaced by service stations, and dealer networks were established by the car manufacturers. By 1939 the car had become an integral part of British life.

However, our view of the cars of the

3

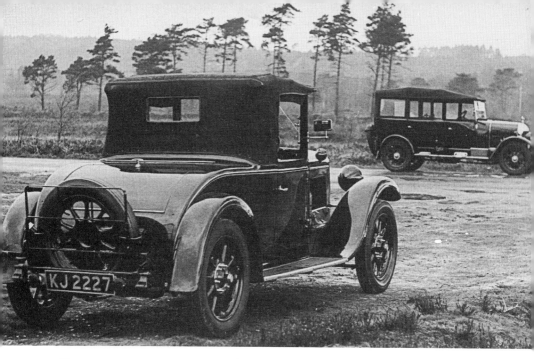

The transition which took place between 1930 and 1940 is clearly visible from these two illustrations. The 1931 Austin 12 with dickey seat, artillery wheels and soft top (above) is only a little more developed than the 'Bullnose' Morris of the 1920s. In contrast, the 1939 Sunbeam Talbot 10 horsepower sports saloon, seen alongside a Vauxhall of the same period (below), shows the progress made in design over the decade.

The first bypasses were constructed to relieve traffic congestion in market towns where road layouts had changed little since medieval times. Their effect was to encourage ribbon development of adjoining land by builders and industrialists, which soon nullified the benefits of improved traffic flow. This is the Kingston Bypass, Surrey, one of the first major roads to be built of reinforced concrete.

1930s can be misleading. A great many were of poor quality and some were downright bad, both in conception and construction. Most have been scrapped or have just rusted away. The survivors are usually the luxury and sports cars, which were mostly hand-built in limited numbers, and frequently uneconomically. Moreover, British cars were not generally of worldwide technical or commercial interest. The driving force during the period came from the United States, where, despite the economic recession, production was vastly greater and technical innovations were marketed long before European manufacturers copied them.

Surprisingly, British cars were comparatively little used abroad, even in the British Empire, other than by bureaucrats and the very wealthy. Price, the availability of servicing and suitability favoured American cars, from Ford to Cadillac, at a time when one pound sterling exchanged for five US dollars.

Only after the Second World War did British manufacturers fully exploit the export market. Not only did the Americans sell worldwide, but they also established factories in Europe, Asia and Australia, frequently working with local manufacturers such as Vauxhall in England, Opel in Germany and Mathis in France.

The automobile industry was largely nationalist and protected itself in a variety of ways. In the United States only a few luxury cars were imported: foreign manufacturers of standard models were unable to compete with the price of home products. The French imposed a 60 per cent duty on foreign cars and manipulated production in favour of small-engined vehicles by means of a heavy tax on petrol. The Italian tax system, which favoured cars under 1100 cc, that is their own Fiats, was reinforced by petrol priced at twice the level in Britain. The British devised their own taxation system, which influenced engine

The concept of regular servicing was introduced by American manufacturers and equipment was produced to take the mystique out of maintenance. The lady owner of this 1937 Buick coupé is being exhorted by the earnest service manager to change her AC Delco oil-filter cartridges. The mechanic working on the car is using a Commentator engine-tuning unit.

design for the next two decades, based on a notional horsepower tax. A formula, the 'RAC Rating', dictated the basis on which duty was payable, calculated by multiplying the number of cylinders in the engine by the cylinder bore, measured in inches. Since the length of a stroke was, in effect, unlimited, small-bore long-stroke engines carried less tax than large-bore units. For example, a 1½ litre Frazer Nash was rated at 12 horsepower, whilst a 1½ litre Opel, with a large-bore short-stroke engine, was rated at 16 horsepower and thus attracted an extra annual tax of £4.

For the first time, regular servicing became established practice, using a deal-er network. The quality of petrol and oils improved, but frequent decarbonising of the cylinder head was needed, typically at 10,000 mile (16,000 km) intervals. Oils were mainly single grade, so that changes for winter and summer were necessary. In cold weather an extended warm-up was necessary if damage to the engine bearing surfaces was to be avoided. Tyres were of large diameter and narrow section. They were more reliable than before but still wore out quickly compared with modern tyres.

The 1930s car featured improved controls and accessories. Lighting was universally electric. The electric starter ceased to be an extra and windscreen

Despite the sales potential of the Empire, British manufacturers were not export-orientated. Popular home models were short-lived on primitive road surfaces abroad and were frequently unable to operate under the extremes of temperature and weather encountered. Status vehicles for the wealthy and the administrators, however, were shipped from Britain. Mr Hall, distributor for Rootes in Nyasaland (now Malawi), poses with a 1935 2.8 litre Hillman 20/70.

Although car ownership in Britain was about one per twenty inhabitants, the roads and parking facilities were very inadequate. This concrete car park at Paignton, Devon, was much admired. A 1936 Rover 10, a Morris 12, several Fords and an SS are parked here.

A typical driver's view of the road. The windscreen can be opened by the handle in the centre of the dashboard to assist ventilation and on some cars it could be opened right up to give better visibility in fog. Instrumentation is comprehensive — the quadrant cluster contains petrol, oil-pressure and water-temperature gauges, plus an ammeter — but warning lights can also be seen. The two large knobs each side raise the windscreen wipers into the operating position. The car is a 1939 Standard Flying Twelve model, with the automobile historian Michael Sedgwick at the wheel.

wipers became standard. The cockpit layout was refined: gear levers tended to be placed in the centre of the front seating compartment; throttle pedals were moved from the centre to the right. Instrumentation became simplified, with warning lights sometimes replacing dials.

The outward appearance of the car changed, influenced greatly by American stylists. No longer was the front grille necessarily a means of cooling and one of the last links with the horse-drawn coach, the running board, was being discarded by the end of the decade. New materials — synthetic fabrics, plastics, perspex and painted metal — replaced the leather and wood used by traditional coachbuilders. Chromium plate was substituted for

nickel and brass. Some of these innovations were not successful. They became shoddy, and as corrosion-resistance technology was in its infancy — particularly on welded steel constructions — trapped mud and water quickly took their toll.

The motor industry rationalised itself during the 1930s. In Britain several major groups became established, including Nuffield (Morris, MG, Wolseley and Riley), Rootes (Humber, Hillman, Sunbeam and British Talbot) and BSA, the armaments manufacturer, which incorporated Daimler and Lanchester, while Rolls-Royce took over Bentley. Nonetheless, there were approximately forty different British makes available,

Ford moved their English factory from Trafford Park, Manchester, to Dagenham, Essex, in the early 1930s. This 1939 photograph shows the 8 and 10 horsepower Ford Prefect production line. Although totally British in concept, the rear-hinged alligator bonnet reveals American influence. The Prefect sold for just under £120.

The 1936 Austin Ruby model represented the ultimate development of the Seven. Many refinements were incorporated, although braking, as the minute drums indicate, was not its strongest feature.

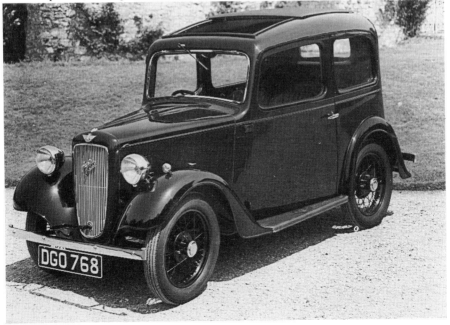

although the days of the medium-sized mass-producer were numbered. A similar pattern occurred in the USA, where Ford (producing Lincoln and Mercury), General Motors (Chevrolet, Cadillac, Packard, Oldsmobile, Buick and La Salle) and Chrysler (Dodge and De Soto) dominated the industry. They produced nearly 3.5 million cars in 1936, compared with British output of only 200,000. In Germany, Audi, DKW, Horch and Wanderer combined to form Auto Union.

Not only were there many makes, but new models were introduced frequently and several manufacturers offered complete ranges of vehicles, large and small, from utility to luxury. Competition was fierce, with the world economic recession easing only at the end of the decade, and prices, particularly for popular models, were pared to the minimum. The car buyer of the 1930s seemed to have the best of all worlds.

THE BRITISH POPULAR CAR

By the end of the 1920s, the principal British popular makes had become established: Austin, whose Seven introduced many people to motoring; Morris, whose Oxford and Cowley models had a solid dependability; and Ford, who quickly realised that their successful American models required considerable adaptation for the British market.

Austin offered a series of models from 750 cc to 2½ litres. These were modified at regular intervals. The Seven was refined, to the detriment of its weight, but its comfort was much improved and technical developments were introduced, such as synchromesh gearboxes and a third main bearing to the crankshaft. The Seven continued in production throughout the decade and the engine design was eventually used to power the three-wheel Reliant. Austin's larger popular model, the 10/4, also remained in production during the 1930s, selling over 100,000, while derivations, such as the six-cylinder Goodwood, were also good sellers.

Morris remained very much in the 1920s tradition, producing models competitive with the Austin range, based on well tried four- and six-cylinder engines. In 1934, however, the introduction of the 919 cc side-valve Morris Eight changed their fortunes, selling over 250,000 in less

Many popular manufacturers produced chassis suitable for coachbuilding. This Austin Twenty must have appealed to those with aristocratic tastes but more humble pockets. The coachwork was by Gordon of Birmingham and was available in various styles. In later days the big Austins, Morrises and Standards became the transport for countless school sports teams, the necessary equipment being piled on the rear luggage rack.

THE **AUSTIN "TWENTY" "GORDON"**

Enclosed Drive
Landaulette de Luxe
7-SEATER
(COACHBUILT)

The 1935 Morris proved to be very popular. The car was extremely well equipped and included a sliding-head roof. The engine was a 90 by 57 mm 918 cc side-valve with three-speed synchromesh gearbox.

The highly successful late pre-war Morris E, in touring form. The ubiquitous E, with its 918 cc engine, appeared in many guises and was for years used by the Post Office.

than four years. For a short time the open Morris could be purchased for £100 (although the contest to market a £100 saloon car was later won by Ford). The larger Morris cars were also steadily improved and combined respectable performance with a few advanced features such as built-in jacks. In 1939 the Series E Eight was introduced, less box-like than the earlier Eight and incorporating unitary construction. A 10 horsepower version also appeared.

Ford persevered for some years with modified Model As and Bs, assembled in Manchester, but in 1932 the Model Y was introduced specially for the British market. It had a 937 cc side-valve four-cylinder engine and was a simple car with basic suspension and unpredictable road-holding. It could achieve 60 mph (97 km/h), consuming fuel at 35 miles per gallon (12 km per litre). For 1936, the price was set at exactly £100 and over 200,000 were sold. A 10 horsepower

A production Ford. The 1937 Ford Eight featured a 939 cc four-cylinder side-valve engine and was available not only in the classic Ford black, but also in blue. The Eight was named the Anglia after the Second World War.

The substantial radiator grilles of cars of the period frequently concealed less than impressive power units. The 1932 10 horsepower Hillman Minx had a four-cylinder 63 mm bore by 95 mm stroke engine cooled by a huge thermo-siphon system. The belt-driven dynamo and coil ignition are clearly visible, together with the horn, mounted incongruously on the cylinder head.

The Hillman Minx was available with various body styles, but the wire wheels and Airline coupé body could not conceal an uninspiring performance.

model was also produced, using the 1172 cc engine later beloved by competitive special builders. Ford's larger models at the end of the 1930s were based on the V8 engine layout so popular in the United States.

The Hillman Minx, introduced by the Rootes brothers in 1931, typified many British cars of the 1930s, with a conventional chassis, semi-elliptic suspension, a four-cylinder side-valve engine, three-speed gearboxes (four on some) and a top speed above 50 mph (80 km/h). The Minx was available in open, coupé or sports form, the last having headlamp grilles, a revolution counter and wire wheels. The sporting image of the Rootes group was enhanced by the acquisition of Talbot and the production of the Talbot 10 (subsequently to become the Sunbeam Talbot).

Standard produced much the same formula, developing from conventional Nines and Tens to more stylish models,

The range of 1933 Standards on show at Wadham Brothers' showrooms at Southsea, Hampshire. Prominent on the right is an SSII Swallow-bodied model, one of William Lyons's first motor cars. On the left, at £159, is a Little Nine.

As the motor car became an essential part of daily life, manufacturers realised the importance of all-weather reliability. A 1939 Vauxhall 10 is the subject of a low-temperature test in their Luton factory cold-room. Despite the total General Motors input, Vauxhall retained the bonnet flutes introduced by Lawrence Pomeroy over twenty years earlier.

including the Flying Standards, and updated body designs with engines ranging from 1100 cc to 2.7 litres. Many Standard components were incorporated into the first SS Jaguars, William Lyons's luxurious saloons, selling at the extremely low price of £385 in 1936.

Singer preferred overhead-valve and overhead-camshaft engines. Although these were more expensive, Singer produced a range of Nine, Ten and Twelve horsepower models, the engines also being used for a successful range of sports cars. They were unable to offer anything

At £565, the Lanchester 15-18 was priced at the top end of the popular market. Featuring the fluid-flywheel transmission shared with Daimler, the Lanchester was a smooth-running, respectable but uninspiring machine.

Respectability in 1936. Skinner's Garage of St Leonards, East Sussex, offered chauffeur-driven Humbers and Hillmans. On show are a 26.8 horsepower Humber Snipe, a Humber Pullman and a Hillman Hawk, all of 1936. With Shell, National Benzol and Cleveland petrols on sale, and Castrol and Mobil lubricants, the day of the tied garage was yet to come.

not already available more cheaply from Morris and the others, however, and the company came under increasing financial pressure.

A major newcomer was Vauxhall, which had previously made high-quality sports cars, such as the Prince Henry, designed by Lawrence Pomeroy, and also later the 30/98. The company had become part of General Motors, who developed their cars for the popular market. The American influence was strong: in 1935 their six-cylinder model was fitted with independent suspension. In 1938 their 10/4 used unitary construction and a highly economical 1200 cc engine, to be followed by 12 and 14 horsepower variants.

Other makers included Jowett, with their flat-four engines, and among the larger cars Rover, Wolseley, Lanchester, Humber and Armstrong Siddeley were popular. Rover predominated with their four- and six-cylinder models, which were conventional, solid and remained in production into the 1950s. Wolseley maintained an up-market image of the Morris, together with production of a sports car, the Hornet. In due course further rationalisation took place within the Nuffield group, the Hornet disappeared and the MG was redesigned to produce a Morris-based sports model. Wolseley became identified with police cars at this time, because the police used the six-cylinder NF model.

Armstrong Siddeley featured pre-selector gearboxes and engines of between 2 and 3 litres fitted into traditional chassis and bodies. Humber, on the other hand, had engines of various capacities, up to the 4 litre Pullman. The big Humbers retailed from £340 to nearly £1000, forming a stepping stone to the luxury cars of the time.

The 1939 Fiat 500 with four-seater cabriolet body, which was produced for the British market only. It was more refined in coachwork than the Italian product.

AMERICAN AND EUROPEAN CARS

Although the major producers of cars in this period were the American manufacturers, there were also sizable industries in Germany, France and Italy and most other European nations had their own producers, who concentrated on local markets. A tiny industry was setting up in Japan.

The American market was dominated by General Motors, Ford and Chrysler. General Motors' major seller was the six-cylinder Chevrolet; they also had the prestige Cadillac, as well as the Oldsmobile, Packard, Buick and La Salle. The 'Chevvy' had a 3 to 3½ litre push-rod overhead-valve engine and was steadily improved during the decade by the fitting of hydraulic brakes and independent suspension (which Rolls-Royce copied) as well as styling. Ford retained cart-spring suspension but their simple four-cylinder power unit was supplemented by the powerful and popular V8. Their up-market marque was the Lincoln, but this was unable to challenge the Cadillac, whose twelve- and sixteen-cylinder cars represented the best on offer in the USA, at a fraction of the price of an imported Rolls-Royce. Chrysler had six- and straight eight-cylinder engines, the latter used in their 4 litre CD model. The Chrysler Airflow model was notable as the forerunner of American styling.

The American cars reflected the low price of fuel and the improvement in the nation's highways, which enabled long journeys to be made and demanded cars with reliable engineering. Overdrives, freewheels and automatic transmission were developed for long, and frequently tedious, journeys: the results were soft-riding designs with cruising speeds of up to 80 mph (130 km/h). This combination of reliability and ride proved popular in overseas countries with primitive roads, notably British Empire territories in Africa, Asia and Australia.

Imports of American cars into Britain were small, partly because of their size, petrol consumption and the heavy road-tax duty payable. General Motors acquired Vauxhall (as well as Opel in Germany) and Ford established manufacturing plants at Dagenham and Cologne and combined with Mathis in France. Chrysler modified their home models for the British market at their Kew factory, using small-bore engines. On a smaller scale, a specialist industry grew up producing British sporting cars powered by American Hudson, Ford, Nash and Lin-

A French four-seater: the 1938 Peugeot 2020 Berline four-door saloon. Its 1133 cc engine and three-speed gearbox were unable to match the sophisticated lines. The central mounting of the headlamps behind the radiator grille to protect them from flying stones was a feature of the period. The artistic design of the front bumper had rather less technical merit.

The Chrysler showrooms in Kew, London, 1933. Chrysler and Plymouth cars were marketed under the Chrysler name and adapted for the British market, even to the extent of refitting conventional cart springs instead of independent front suspension. In the foreground is a 33 horsepower Imperial Eight, with a Kew Six alongside in chassis form. A complete Kew Six can be seen in the centre background.

The 1350 cc Lancia Aprilia of 1937. The rear torsion-bar suspension supplemented the traditional Lancia sliding-pillar front springing. The engine block was aluminium and the car had a good performance of 0 to 30 mph (0 to 50 km/h) in 6.1 seconds.

coln engines. Some of the best known results of this combination were Railton, Jensen, Brough Superior, Raymond Mays and Allard.

In Italy politics and the depression favoured the small 1100 cc Fiat. This company in 1936 produced the Topolino, a 500 cc four-seater which not only reached 55 mph (88 km/h) but ran 50 miles (80 km) on a gallon of petrol. Lancia made larger touring cars but their best known model was the Aprilia, introduced in 1936, the torsion-bar rear suspension of which set remarkable road-holding standards. The body of the Aprilia was very light and the power unit was a 1352 cc aluminium-block overhead-camshaft engine.

Three companies headed the industry in France: Peugeot, Renault and Citroën. The Peugeots were utilitarian rather than exciting. Typically, the 201, of which some 140,000 were produced between 1929 and 1937, was based on an 1100 cc side-valve engine which achieved 0 to 45 mph (0 to 72 km/h) in thirty seconds. The 1460 cc 301 was hardly more exciting, but in 1936 a six-cylinder car with overhead valves coupled to a Cotal electric gearbox and full-width aerodynamic body, the 601, was a much more noteworthy

vehicle. Renault retained a wide range of saloons, coupés and other body styles on cars from 1½ litres to the presidential 7 litre. The Renault 1 litre 6CV with independent suspension was the forerunner of the French economy car of the 1940s and 1950s, but they also made some more exciting models, such as the 4.2 litre Nerva straight eight which won the Monte Carlo Rally in 1935. Citroën produced undistinguished models prior to the introduction in 1934 of the revolutionary *Traction Avant*. Designed as a passenger compartment bolted on behind a power unit complete with transmission, the Citroën's excellence in acceleration and roadholding was such that it became the favourite of smash and grab robbers! Over 700,000 were made during a production run spanning three decades, a limited number of which were built in England at Slough. Four- and six-cylinder engines from 1300 cc upwards were used. In the late 1930s Citroën unveiled the 375 cc 2CV, the ultimate in basic cars, with its characteristic 'corrugated iron' body. The war temporarily interrupted the development of this totally French car, which nearly fifty years later achieved cult status.

Production in Germany also covered a

18

The 1935 Renault ADC 1 Celtaquatre, a two- to four-seater of 1½ litres capacity, which could achieve 60 mph (100 km/h) at nearly 50 miles per gallon (17 km per litre).

wide range. Mercedes-Benz specialised in luxury vehicles but entered the popular car market with the 170 and the uncommercial rear-engined 150S. The largest manufacturer was Opel, under General Motors' direction, whose Olympia of 1 to 1½ litre capacity sold over 100,000. The 500 cc twin-cylinder two-stroke DKW

with front-wheel drive sold cheaply, becoming the basis of the post-war Wartburg. Meanwhile, Germany under the Third Reich was becoming a motoring nation. The passing of the Depression and the construction of the autobahn system of purpose-built motor roads led to the design of a 'people's car'. Adler

Traction Avant. The confusingly titled 1939 Citroën 11 (B16 Fifteen) in right-hand drive form. Note the very large passenger compartment, uncluttered by a transmission tunnel or gear lever, the mechanism of which projected through the dashboard. Until the advent of the Mini, the Citroën was, by far the most successful front-wheel drive vehicle produced.

and others produced proposals but the honour fell to Dr Ferdinand Porsche and the Volkswagen. Military priorities meant that only two hundred cars were produced before the outbreak of war. The basic concept of a light (12½ cwt, 640 kg) vehicle with 1 litre air-cooled horizontally opposed overhead-valve four-cylinder engine mounted at the rear and with torsion-bar rear suspension remained unchanged. The design and concept of the Volkswagen was subsequently dismissed as being of no significance by the Allied engineers in 1946. Perhaps they were frightened by the cable brakes initially fitted.

BMW produced a series of saloons from 1933 based on a small six-cylinder overhead-valve engine. This rapidly rose to 1½ and then to 2 litre capacity. In 1936, set on a box chassis with modern styling, independent front suspension, torsion-bar rear suspension and hydraulic brakes, the BMW engine produced a series of excellent saloons and tourers, culminating in the classic 328 sports car.

The fledgling motor industry in Japan was nearly strangled by bureaucracy. American cars were assembled locally but the first notable local product was a 500 cc Datsun with strong similarities to the Austin Seven, while Toyota produced a 3.4 litre saloon with American antecedents.

This 1937 prototype Volkswagen, designed by Dr Ferdinand Porsche, was the forerunner of the most famous of all popular cars. Initially it needed much refining, even lacking synchromesh gears. By the time the Allies took over after the Second World War, it was still largely unproven, but the British motor industry must have regretted their inability to spot a good thing in the making. Note the curious little front luggage boot and front-opening doors of the prototype.

Racing car in miniature. The six-cylinder supercharged 1087 cc K3 MG. Designed and constructed in six weeks, it was probably the finest of Cecil Kimber's creations, winning its class in the Mille Miglia and the Tourist Trophy outright, with Tazio Nuvolari at the wheel.

SPORTS CARS

The 1930s marked a high point for the sports car. Never before had there been so much choice, which fell broadly into three categories and price ranges.

The manufacture of cheap mass-produced sports cars (under £250) was led by Austin, who offered performance motoring for as little as £150, using the formula developed for the Austin Seven, a 747 cc engine with a three-speed gearbox in a simple chassis. MG, on the other hand, created increasingly sophisticated designs with a strong association between production and competition models. The overhead-camshaft R design was a racing car in miniature. Singer, trading on competition success, introduced their Le Mans range in 1935 and Wolseley's Hornets provided a sporting image at least. With few exceptions, the cheaper cars were constrained by cost, usually featuring steel bodies with attendant corrosion and extra weight.

Austin dropped production of sports cars in 1938 and the specialist approach by MG under Cecil Kimber disappeared in the 1936 Nuffield reorganisation. Thereafter MG produced attractive but pedestrian cars, such as the early T series, which drew heavily on stock Morris parts, together with some up-market sports saloons.

At the other end of the range, at £1000 and more, Bentley, acquired by Rolls-Royce in 1931, Alvis, Lagonda and Talbot all produced hand-made quality performance sports cars and high-speed tourers. The characteristics included lowered chassis, emphasising length, smooth lines and a much greater degree of comfort than their 1920s predecessors. This was often achieved at the expense of weight, roadholding and acceleration; however, roads were much improved, both in width and gradient, so that, once reached, top speeds of around 90 mph (145 km/h) could be maintained. The quality sports-car manufacturers normally produced a chassis, which was then fitted with a body to the customer's requirements by a coachbuilder. Alloys and sometimes steel were used, stretched over wooden framework, ash being preferred on account of its flexural strength.

The last great Bentley, the 8 litre, was discontinued by Rolls-Royce and replaced by 3½ and later 4½ litres. Competitive activities were discouraged and,

The perfect traditional British sports car. The 1½ litre HRG, powered by the 4ED Meadows engine, made few concessions to comfort. This particular car, with cycle wings and extended tail, won its class in the 1939 24 Hour Le Mans race, driven by Peter Clark and Marcus Chambers.

at £1500 in 1936, the Bentley appealed to a limited clientele. Throughout the 1930s Lagonda built up a sporting reputation with 2, 3 and 4½ litre models, including a win at Le Mans in 1935. The same year W. O. Bentley left Rolls-Royce and joined Lagonda to design a V12 4½ litre engine which powered both production machines and Lagonda's 1939 prototype sports racers. The Rootes brothers rationalised Talbot, but not before Georges Roesch had created the splendid 90 and 105 models, both formidable all-round competition cars. The 105, suitably prepared, could lap Brooklands,

Britain's premier race circuit, at around 130 mph (209 km/h).

The continental manufacturers mostly produced expensive high-performance machines, frequently racing cars modified for road use. Alfa Romeo's 6C 2.3 litre and 8C 2.9 litre were typical, the latter being based on the famous twin overhead-camshaft Grand Prix P3 model. The 2.3 litre Maserati was also fundamentally a Grand Prix car, as was the Bugatti Type 55, now the most desirable of all the sports cars produced at Molsheim. However, the 3.3 litre Type 57, with many superb and advanced body-

Talbot's most notable products were the 90 and 105 models, featuring the six-cylinder engine designed by Georges Roesch. This is a 1931 Offord-bodied 90. Note the unusual rear bumper configuration to cope with the pointed tail.

22

The effect of aerodynamics on high-speed car design was apparent in the late 1930s, notably among the European manufacturers, with Bugatti and Alfa Romeo to the fore. This is type 8C 2900B Alfa coupé, driven by Sommer and Biondetti in the 1938 Le Mans 24 Hour race.

The 2 litre BMW Type 328 was a remarkable all-round sports car which had many competition successes. Sold in Britain as the Frazer Nash BMW, it could achieve 100 mph (160 km/h). Its cross push-rod six-cylinder engine became the basis for many post-war British sports and racing cars, including Bristol, Frazer Nash and Cooper.

The 1934 Type 55 2.3 litre Bugatti with fixed-head coupé body designed by Jean Bugatti. These machines were essentially racing cars adapted for the road and were supplied in supercharged and unsupercharged form. Some 38 Type 55s were built at the Bugatti factory at Molsheim in Alsace. The classic Bugatti cast-alloy wheels, integral with the brake drums, are prominent.

Fiat's Turin-manufactured 508S Balilla models were popular in competition. Using 1100 and 1500 cc four-cylinder engines, Fiats became the basis of several other marques. The 508S was also manufactured under licence as the NSU-Fiat and the car on the right is a German-produced car.

Adrian Squire built just six 1.5 litre Anzani-engined Squires at a small factory in Remenham, near Henley-on-Thames, Oxfordshire. The Duke of Grafton ordered this one as a racing car in 1935, but it was converted to a nominal two-seater sports-car configuration shortly afterwards.

Aston Martin manufactured 1.5 and 2 litre sports models throughout the 1930s, achieving considerable competition success, albeit under continuous financial difficulties. This is a rare fixed-head coupé version. The front suspension is typical of the period, featuring semi-elliptic springs with transverse friction shock-absorbers. The brakes are operated by cables adjusted from the front, and the clam-shell wings are mounted on the brake backplates to turn with the wheels. Behind the Aston is a 4½ litre saloon Lagonda.

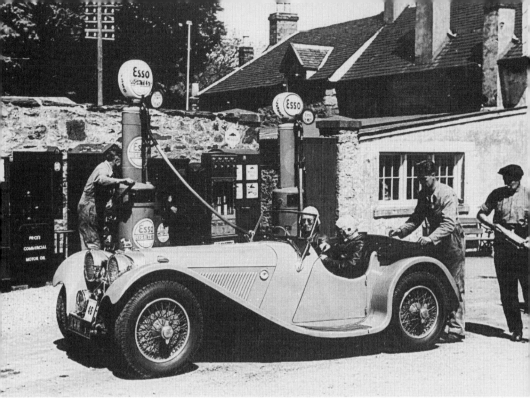

Filling up at a typical village garage during the Scottish Rally. Note the hand-operated pumps and the oil and cigarette dispensers. The car is an SS100 and the occupants are in period headwear. Regular petrol was 1s 6d and premium grade 1s 8d per gallon.

To the 1930s public motor racing and Brooklands were synonymous, featuring both the racing aces and many club events. This 1936 photograph shows the start of a timed speed event in which passengers could be carried. Some twenty different marques are visible, notably Austin, MG, Fiat and Aston Martin.

Three wheels remained popular as an economic means of open-sports motoring. The Super Sports Morgan was essentially a competition car, while its more prosaic equivalent on the right was designed for family motoring and it is not difficult to imagine its conversion into a four-wheel model.

work styles, sold in much greater numbers. Other French manufacturers, notably Delahaye, who merged with Delage, and the French Talbot company, also greatly enhanced their productions using body design by Figoni and Falaschi and by Saoutchik.

Two other notable continental producers were BMW and Fiat. BMW, who had previously produced family cars, introduced a range of open and closed sports cars, culminating in the 328, a genuine 100 mph (160 km/h) 2 litre, the engine of which became the basic power unit for many post-war single-seaters. Fiat achieved success with 1100 cc and 1500 cc Balilla models, which in their turn became the basis for Simca, Cisitalia and Gordini.

The middle price range, between £300 and £750, was dominated by British 1½ and 2 litre cars. These were produced in

Apart from circuit racing, rallying and trials were very popular, attracting large entries and becoming at times a public nuisance. This is the start of the 1938 Scottish Rally in Edinburgh, featuring a 1934 9 horsepower coupé Singer, a 1937 1.5 litre ex-works team Singer and a new SS Jaguar saloon.

limited numbers mainly by small companies on tight budgets. Engines and components were frequently bought-out items from Meadows, ENV, Moss and others, but the end results differed widely. Notable among the 1100 cc class were the Riley Nine and the twin overhead-camshaft Lagonda Rapier. Riley also produced 1½ litre four- and six-cylinder models, the six engine forming the basis of the ERA racing car. Riley's Imp, Sprite and MPH were classic open sports cars but many components were shared with sports saloons such as the Kestrel and Adelphi with their characteristic streamlined body styling.

Frazer Nash and HRG produced traditional designs, similar in concept, but with the Frazer Nash retaining its chain-driven transmission. Both had flexible chassis with light bodies and minimal suspension, giving remarkable roadholding. They relied heavily on the 1½ litre Meadows 4ED engine. In the late 1930s Frazer Nash associated with BMW, while HRG drew up plans for a highly advanced range, but these were unfulfilled. Rare and very desirable was the 1½ litre Anzani-engined Squire, but the class was dominated by Aston Martin

and their fast but heavy Ulster, International and Le Mans models. A wide range of body styles was offered, two- and four-seater, open and closed, and latterly 2 litre models were added. Aston Martin enjoyed extensive competition success, but many other marques, such as AC, were more suitable for high-speed touring. A newcomer in 1936 was the SS100, effectively the first Jaguar sports car, powered by a 2663 cc six-cylinder engine manufactured by Standard. Its roadholding was not exemplary, but it had pace and a great deal of grace, all for £395.

Three-wheeler enthusiasts were well catered for. Morgan's air-cooled motorcycle-powered machines remained in production throughout the decade, although the introduction of the Coventry Climax-engined four-wheel 4/4 in 1936 pointed the way to the future. BSA also manufactured three- and four-wheel cars.

A schedule of sports cars available on the British market in 1936 listed some forty makes and ninety models, ranging from £142 to over £2000 and from under 750 cc to over 5 litres. At the same date, a second-hand Bugatti retailed for under £50.

The Phantom III Rolls-Royce, with its 7.3 litre V12 engine, was introduced in 1935, setting new standards in artsuncrule motoring A Phantom III cost some £3000 and petrol consumption was around 10 miles per gallon (3.5 km per litre), supplied for a 33 gallon (150 litre) tank. The coachbuilder in this instance was Hooper.

Despite the prestige of Rolls-Royce, Daimlers were much used by royalty, frequently with coachwork by Barker, who held the royal warrant. Queen Mary had a 50 horsepower model. This 1934 chassis, number 39702, was built up for Mr C. de Beistegui. Despite the cavernous rear compartment, luggage was exposed to the elements. Overall weight depended on the coachwork, but some Daimlers were nearly 2½ tonnes.

CARS FOR THE NOBILITY AND GENTRY

Although the luxury market suffered considerably from the 1929 financial crisis and the consequent Depression, production of prestige cars continued much as in the 1920s.

Daimler retained their dominance of the prestige business, based on their royal warrant. They relied initially on their well tried sleeve-valve engine either in straight-six 3½ litre form or in double-six (in other words V12) configuration, such as the 6½ litre 40/50 model of 1931-5. Although the chassis weighed nearly 2 tonnes, attempts were made to fit open sports bodies but traditional coachbuilder's designs predominated. In the mid 1930s more conventional six- and eight-cylinder overhead-valve engines of up to 4½ litres were introduced and throughout this period fluid-flywheel transmission was offered, all adding to the smoothness of the ride. Small Daimlers and Lanchesters, both products of the BSA group, were also available.

The flagship of the Rolls-Royce factory at Derby was the Phantom II with a 7.6 litre six-cylinder overhead-valve engine. Lighter than the Daimler, at 1680 kg (33 cwt) chassis weight, its speed was in excess of 80 mph (129 km/h) with a fuel consumption of 11 miles per gallon (4 km per litre). This PII was also available in 'Continental' form for grand touring and capable of extra speed. In 1935 the Phantom III appeared, with a 7.3 litre V12 engine. Essentially a chauffeur-driven car like its predecessor, the PIII provided a major improvement in roadholding by using independent front suspension. Ride control, servo-assisted brakes and hydraulically controlled self-adjusting valve tappets were also featured. Many believe that the PIII was the greatest of all Rolls-Royces. At £3000 it was a substantial investment, and for less formal use the 3.6 litre six-cylinder 20/25 model was offered, followed by the 25/30 and the 4½ litre Wraith, the latter being a scaled-down Phantom III. These two smaller engines, with raised compressions, powered the Rolls Bentleys. The true luxury Bentley of the 1930s, the last designed by W. O. Bentley, was the 1930 six-cylinder 8 litre model, which, despite its magnificence, could achieve 110 mph (177 km/h).

W. O. Bentley returned to this type of

The 1937 Alvis Speed 25. After the 1930s the high-speed quality open tourers tended to disappear from the market. This car retains its exposed wire wheels, but many makers covered the spokes with discs, as seen on the Bentley.

motor car in 1935, designing the V12 4½ litre Lagonda, which was both a luxury and a sports car. The sleek body was not designed to offer the total comfort of the Daimler and Rolls but its smooth performance and advanced suspension were ahead of its time. Alvis also produced a range of luxury sporting saloons based on their '20' and '25' open models.

The major European challenger to the British in this field was Mercedes Benz. Whilst their racing success during the 1930s was legendary, Mercedes concentrated on the production of high-quality limousines. In 1930 the Grosser, a 7.7 litre supercharged model weighing over 2½ tonnes, was introduced, to be replaced in 1933 by a more sophisticated version, the straight-eight 380K, with all-independent suspension. This was followed by similar eight-cylinder cars such as the 500K and the 540K, culminating in the 580K, which was capable of over 130 mph (208 km/h), in 1939.

People with a little less finance preferred prestige products from the United States, such as the Lincolns, Packards and Cadillacs, whose eight-, twelve- and sixteen-cylinder cars were magnificent. Edward VIII owned a Canadian-built Buick.

American luxury cars came finished, but most British customers bought their cars in chassis form and then had bodies constructed to their taste by one of some fifty established coachbuilders. Daimler, Rolls-Royce and Bentley provided chassis ready for this process but almost any make could be obtained in this form. Many people used famous firms such as the two Mulliners, Park Ward, Barker, James Young, and Freestone and Webb. One coachbuilder particularly associated with the period was Gurney Nutting, who catered for the younger members of the Royal Family and Indian potentates.

Once the design was agreed, full-scale templates were cut and construction commenced on an ash-wood frame. This would then be covered in an aluminium or steel skin. The use of metal, which permitted curvilinear designs, largely superseded fabric. Traditional joinery techniques were employed for the frame, a notable exception being the Weymann-patented design, whose plate joints permitted considerable flexing. The more advanced car designs featured long sweeping tails and wings. In many cases the rear wheels were totally enclosed. Another trend was in the design of the doors to give one continuous side win-

After their acquisition by Rolls-Royce in 1931, Bentleys were built as luxury open cars with some sporting pretensions. This 1935 3½ litre six-cylinder sedanca de ville appears more suited to weekend golfing than competitive driving.

American style — the 1935 6.8 litre Model K Lincoln in suitably palatial surroundings. Compared with European competitors, the Lincoln was inexpensive, at around £1000 on the road, but, despite the almost total lack of chrome plate, most American cars were regarded as 'flashy', particularly those with white-walled tyres.

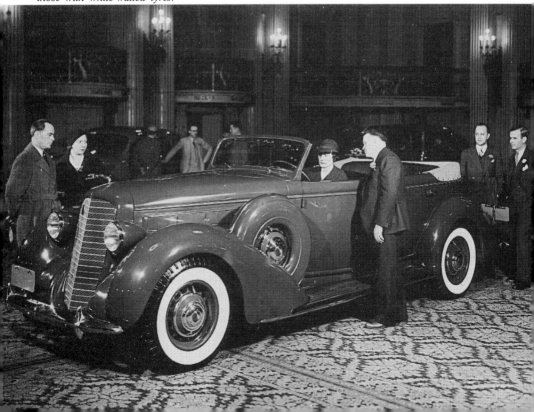

dow. New materials, such as perspex, were also used experimentally.

Interiors were fitted out to the highest standards. Burr walnut veneers (some coachbuilders kept matched panels for customers in case of accident), inlaid metal and fittings such as cocktail cabinets were *de rigueur*. Other interesting refinements included the Brooks suitcase, a detachable unit designed as part of the car which, when opened, revealed a set of tailor-made leather luggage cases.

Lighting was much improved and many makes featured large Lucas P100 headlights, with various dipping mechanisms. Barkers even designed swivelling units. At night rear window blinds could be raised to eliminate glare and other refinements included effective heaters, radios and thermos-flask holders. For the well-off customer there was little the luxury manufacturer and coachbuilder could not provide.

FURTHER READING

Boddy, William. *Continental Sports Cars*. Foulis, 1951.
Demaus, A. B. *Motoring in the Thirties and Forties*. Batsford, 1979.
Grant, Gregor. *British Sports Cars*. Foulis, 1947.
Scott Moncrieff, David. *The Thoroughbred Motor Car 1930-1940*. Batsford, 1963.
Sedgwick, Michael. *Cars of the Thirties*. Batsford, 1970.
Sedgwick, Michael. *Cars of the Thirties and Forties*. Hamlyn, 1979.
Wheatley, Richard, and Morgan, Brian. *The Restoration of Vintage and Thoroughbred Cars*. Batsford, 1957.

Individual histories of most of the marques described in this album are also available. The monthly journals *Motor Sport*, *The Automobile*, *Classic Car* and *Classic and Sports Car* regularly feature articles on cars and motoring in the 1930s and also list relevant one-make clubs.

PLACES TO VISIT

Intending visitors are advised to check the dates and times of opening before making a special journey.

Doune Motor Museum, Carse of Cambus, Doune, Perthshire FK16 6HA. Telephone: 0786 841203.
Heritage Motor Museum, Syon Park, Brentford, Middlesex TW8 3JF. Telephone: 01-560 1378.
Midland Motor Museum, Stanmore Hall, Stourbridge Road, Bridgnorth, Shropshire WV15 5JG. Telephone: 0746 761761.
National Motor Museum, John Montagu Building, Beaulieu, Brockenhurst, Hampshire SO4 7ZN. Telephone: 0590 612345.
Totnes Motor Museum, Steamer Quay, Totnes, Devon TQ9 5AL. Telephone: 0803 862777.

Many displays and *concours* are held throughout Great Britain, particularly in the summer months. Some 1930s cars, described as 'post-vintage thoroughbreds', are eligible to compete in races, driving tests and other events organised by the Vintage Sports Car Club. Frequently the cars in the car parks at such meetings are as interesting as those competing! Details of these and similar gatherings are published in the journals.